W9-AAZ-678

ANGLERFISH

A Buddy Book by
Deborah Coldiron

ABDO
Publishing Company

UNDERWATER
WORLD

VISIT US AT
www.abdopublishing.com

Published by ABDO Publishing Company, 8000 West 78th Street, Edina, Minnesota 55439.

Printed in the United States.

Coordinating Series Editor: Sarah Tieck
Contributing Editor: Michael P. Goecke
Graphic Design: Deborah Coldiron
Cover Photograph: Visuals Unlimited: E. Widder/HBOI
Interior Photographs/Illustrations: Clipart.com (pages 9, 25); Corbis (page 13, 23); ImageMix (page 7, 13, 15, 19, 21); Minden Pictures: David Shale/npl (page 11), Norbert Wu (pages 17, 19, 27); Photos.com (pages 5, 18, 19, 23); T. W. Pietsch, University of Washington (page 30); Jeff Rotman Photography (page 18); Wikipedia Commons: Carl Chun (page 25)

Library of Congress Cataloging-in-Publication Data

Coldiron, Deborah
    Anglerfish / Deborah Coldiron.
       p. cm. — (Underwater world)
    Includes index.
    ISBN 978-1-59928-819-2
     1. Anglerfishes—Juvenile literature. I. Title.

    QL637.9.L6C65 2007
    597'.62—dc22

                          2007016265

Table Of Contents

The World Of Anglerfish

Every living creature needs water. Some animals not only need water, they live in it, too.

Scientists have found more than 250,000 kinds of plants and animals living underwater. And, they believe there could be one million more! The anglerfish is one animal that makes its home in this underwater world.

Seventy percent of Earth's surface is covered in water.

Anglerfish are best known for the clever way they capture their prey. Their body has what looks like a fishing pole and a lure.

The smallest anglerfish is less than one-quarter inch (.64 cm) long. The largest may grow up to six feet (2 m) in length.

Some anglerfish are found in warm, coastal waters. Others live in the deep, dark sea.

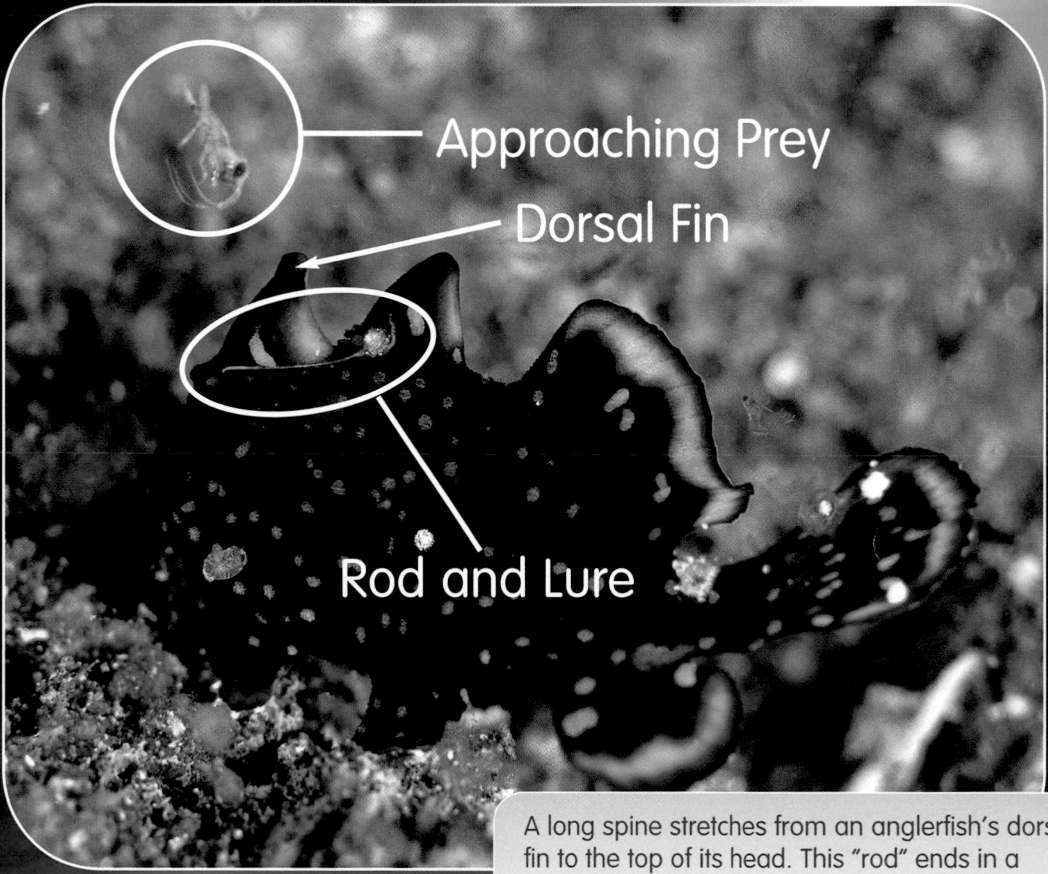

Approaching Prey

Dorsal Fin

Rod and Lure

A long spine stretches from an anglerfish's dorsal fin to the top of its head. This "rod" ends in a growth of flesh that acts as a lure to bait prey.

Ready For A Close-Up?

There are around 200 known **species** of anglerfish. These species can be grouped into four basic types. These are batfish, deep-sea anglerfish, frogfish, and goosefish.

Anglerfish have very large heads and relatively small bodies. Their mouths are very wide. So, some anglerfish have the nickname "allmouth."

If a fish bites off an anglerfish's lure, it's not a problem. These adaptive creatures can grow a new one!

Four Basic Anglerfish Types

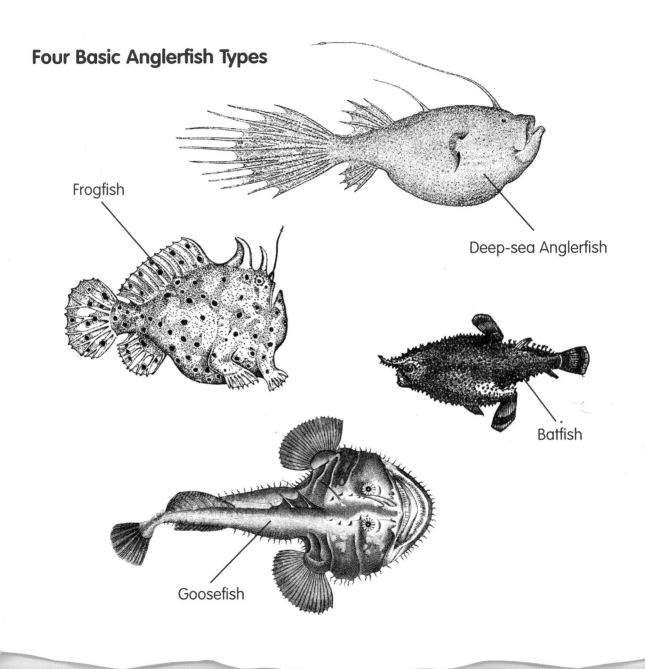

Frogfish

Deep-sea Anglerfish

Batfish

Goosefish

Anglerfish are usually well camouflaged, or hidden. Often when anglerfish rest on the seafloor, only their lures can be seen.

The spine that forms the anglerfish's rod is called an illicium. The lure, or **bait**, is called an esca. Some esca are **bioluminescent**. And, many esca are shaped like small marine animals. They may look like shrimp, marine worms, or small fish.

Deep-sea anglerfish live far beneath the ocean's surface where no sunlight reaches. These anglerfish have bioluminescent esca to attract prey.

Most anglerfish live near the ocean floor. And, many are poor swimmers. Some anglerfish use their fins as legs! They use two or four fins to slowly walk on the seafloor.

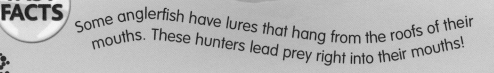

FAST FACTS Some anglerfish have lures that hang from the roofs of their mouths. These hunters lead prey right into their mouths!

Frogfish are one example of anglerfish that use their fins as legs.

A Growing Anglerfish

An anglerfish begins life in a tiny egg. When anglerfish eggs hatch, the larvae are small. And, they are usually transparent, or see-through.

Some anglerfish larvae can swim and hunt right away. Others drift near the ocean surface with other tiny creatures known as **plankton**. Eventually, they sink down to the seafloor to live.

FAST FACTS

Anglerfish eggs contain large oil droplets that help the eggs float to the ocean surface.

Young anglerfish usually look like small adult anglerfish.

Partners For Life

Some male and female deep-sea anglerfish have interesting relationships. They live in dark, lonely waters. So, some have found a way to make sure they are together to **spawn**.

Many males are tiny compared to females. When a male finds a female, he attaches himself to her body. So, when the female spawns, the male is available to **fertilize** her eggs.

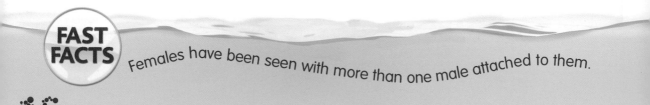

FAST FACTS Females have been seen with more than one male attached to them.

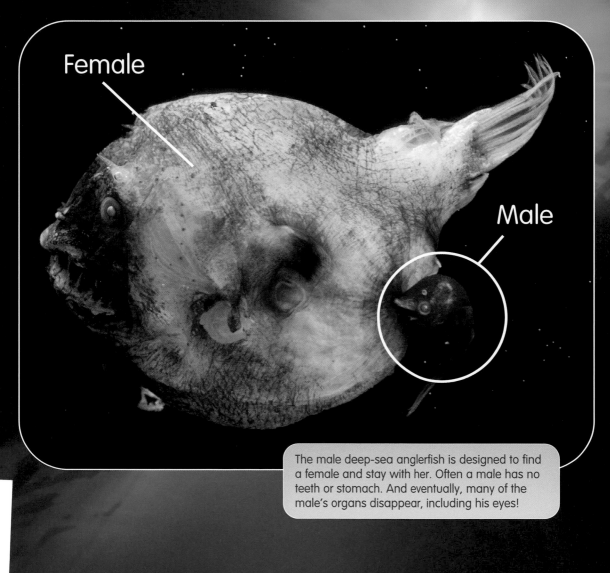

Female

Male

The male deep-sea anglerfish is designed to find a female and stay with her. Often a male has no teeth or stomach. And eventually, many of the male's organs disappear, including his eyes!

Family Tree

Goosefish, batfish, frogfish, and deep-sea anglerfish are the four types of anglerfish. They all hunt for food in similar ways. And, many have similar **habitats**.

Sometimes, it is hard to believe these fish are related at all! Even though they all have a lure, these anglerfish look very different.

Goosefish are among the largest anglerfish. Some grow to lengths of about six feet (2 m)! Despite their size, goosefish live in shallow waters and spend much time hidden in sand.

Frogfish walk on two fins and grow to about 12 inches (30 cm) long. They are known for their camouflage abilities. Some can even change their skin color! Such skills help them hide among plants and animals in the shallow waters where they live.

Female deep-sea anglerfish are known for the bright light of their lures. They also have very flexible stomachs. Some females are able to eat meals as big as their own bodies!

Compared to other anglerfish, batfish have relatively small mouths. Batfish grow to about 14 inches (36 cm) long. And unlike other anglerfish, batfish have a small tube on their head. This hides their lure when they aren't using it to hunt.

Hunting For Dinner

Anglerfish are **carnivores**. They eat many different kinds of fish. And, they eat **crustaceans**, such as shrimp.

Anglerfish are very clever hunters. Just like human fishers, they use a sit-and-wait approach to catch dinner.

Anglerfish can stay perfectly still for long periods of time. They often wait for prey to swim by. An anglerfish can strike very quickly when a fish nears its lure!

FAST FACTS

Anglerfish are said to have the fastest bite of any animal that has a backbone. Their bite is so quick that you may not even see it happen!

22

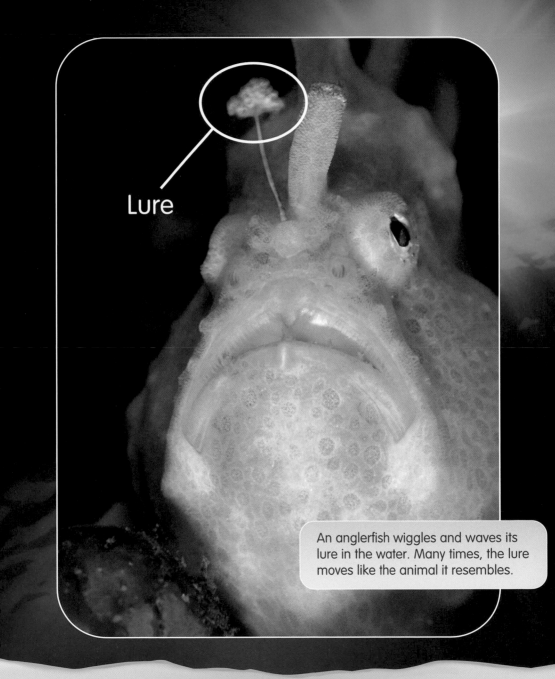

Lure

An anglerfish wiggles and waves its lure in the water. Many times, the lure moves like the animal it resembles.

Home Sweet Home

Most anglerfish live in the deep sea. But some live in warm, coastal waters. Anglerfish that live in shallow waters share their **habitat** with coral and sea sponges. Rays, some sharks, and many fish also share these areas.

FAST FACTS

Some anglerfish have hairlike structures on their bodies that act like sense organs. These allow anglerfish to sense movement in the water nearby.

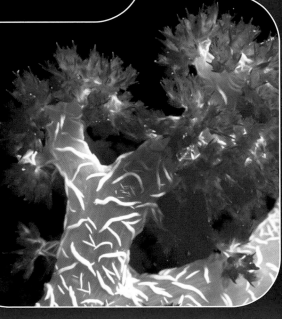

In shallow waters, anglerfish neighbors include rays (*above left*), coral (*above*), and sea sponges (*left*).

On the other hand, deep-sea anglerfish live near many strange and wonderful creatures. Some of their deep-sea neighbors include the gulper eel, the Dumbo octopus, and the vampire squid.

FAST FACTS

Thanks to improvements in underwater exploration, new species of deep-sea animals are constantly being discovered.

Unlike most eels, the gulper's body is not muscular. Its mouth makes up about one-quarter of its body length. The gulper's jaw opens so wide that it can eat an animal as big as itself!

Vampire squid have very large eyes and webbed arms. But, they are not really squid or octopuses.

A Dangerous World

People are the biggest threat to the anglerfish population. Many **environmentalists** are especially concerned about overfishing goosefish.

Another growing threat to deep-sea anglerfish is a type of fishing called trawling. Fishermen are developing new ways to drag trawls, or nets, deeper into the ocean.

Trawling nets trap all kinds of ocean animals. And, they often harm underwater habitats.

Fascinating Facts

➤ The Latin name *Linophrynidae arborifera* means "toad that fishes with a net." This strange deep-sea anglerfish has a lure attached to its head. And it has rootlike **barbels** dangling from its chin.

➤ In many parts of the world, goosefish is considered a tasty treat. The goosefish's tail is called "poor man's lobster."

➤ Some anglerfish have long, whiplike lures. These can be five times longer than their body length. One such deep-sea anglerfish is the *Gigantactis macronema*.

➤ Many anglerfish mothers lay their eggs in very large sheets of **mucus**. These "rafts" may contain up to one million eggs! They can be around three feet (1 m) wide and 25 to 35 feet (8 to 11 m) long. The rafts are not attached to the seafloor. Instead, they float freely in the ocean **currents**.

Learn And Explore

What is the world's smallest fish? Scientists don't all agree.

Ted Pietsch of the University of Washington says it is *Photocorynus spiniceps*. Scientists say this deep-sea anglerfish male measures only about one-quarter inch (.64 cm) long!

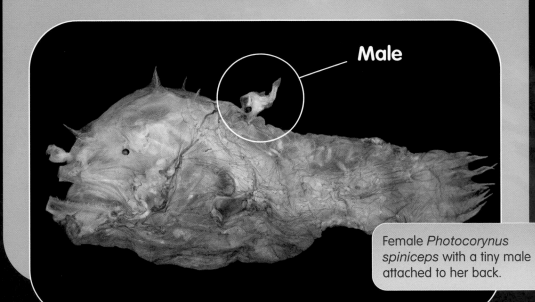

Male

Female *Photocorynus spiniceps* with a tiny male attached to her back.

IMPORTANT WORDS

bait to attract animals. It is also the food put on a hook or in a trap to attract animals.

barbel a fleshy growth dangling near a fish's mouth.

bioluminescent able to give off light.

carnivore a meat-eater.

crustacean any of a group of animals with hard shells that live mostly in water. Crabs, lobsters, and shrimp are all crustaceans.

current the flow and movement of a large body of water.

environmentalist a person who is interested in protecting the natural world.

fertilize able to produce seeds, fruit, or young.

habitat where an animal lives in the wild.

mucus thick, slippery fluid from the body.

plankton a group of very small plants and animals that float in the water. Many animals eat plankton.

spawn to release eggs.

species living things that are very much alike.

WEB SITES

To learn more about anglerfish, visit ABDO Publishing Company on the World Wide Web. Web sites about anglerfish are featured on our Book Links page. These links are routinely monitored and updated to provide the most current information available.

www.abdopublishing.com

INDEX